ROULETTES

The Roulettes were formed in 1970 to celebrate the 50th birthday of the Royal Australian Air Force (RAAF).

ROULETTES

# HIGH FLYERS

SUE WARREN

CREATIVE EDUCATION · CREATIVE PAPERBACKS

Published by Creative Education and Creative Paperbacks
P.O. Box 227, Mankato, Minnesota 56002
Creative Education and Creative Paperbacks are imprints of The Creative Company
www.thecreativecompany.us

Book Design by Graham Morgan
Art direction by Blue Design (www.bluedes.com)

Images by Flickr/Aviatrix, 18; Getty Images/Chris Putnam, 22, Ian Hitchcock, cover, PAUL CROCK, 26, Paul Kitchener, 14; Public Domain, 7; Shutterstock/FiledIMAGE, 12-13; Unsplash/Joshua Brown, 6; Wikimedia Commons/Bidgee, 4-5, 11, 21, 32, Fir0002, 2, FotoSleuth, 29, Robert Frola, 1, 8, 10, 25, 30



Library of Congress Cataloging-in-Publication Data
Names: Warren, Sue (Susan Marjorie), 1956- author.
Title: Roulettes / Sue Warren.
Description: Mankato, Minnesota : Creative Education and Creative Paperbacks, [2026] | Series: High flyers | Includes bibliographical references and index. | Audience: Ages 10-13 | Audience: Grades 4-6 | Summary: "Loops. Rolls. High-G turns. The Royal Australian Air Force Roulettes perform stunning aerial displays. Soar high with the Roulettes in this visually stunning introduction to their history, present, and future, geared toward upper-elementary readers"— Provided by publisher.
Identifiers: LCCN 2025015376 (print) | LCCN 2025015377 (ebook) | ISBN 9798895810651 (library binding) | ISBN 9798896800187 (paperback) | ISBN 9798895811917 (ebook)
Subjects: LCSH: Australia. Royal Australian Air Force. Aerobatic Team—Juvenile literature. | Stunt flying--Australia—Juvenile literature. | Aeronautics, Military—Australia—Juvenile literature. | Air shows—Australia—Juvenile literature. | CYAC: Stunt flying. | Military aeronautics. | Air shows.
Classification: LCC UG632.3.A8 W37 2026 (print) | LCC UG632.3.A8 (ebook) | DDC 797.5/40994—dc23/eng/20250513
LC record available at https://lccn.loc.gov/2025015376
LC ebook record available at https://lccn.loc.gov/2025015377

Printed in the United States

**ABOUT THE AUTHOR** — The daughter of a WWII Lancaster airman, Sue Warren was surrounded by talk and images of fighter planes her entire childhood. She has always maintained an interest in aircraft of all vintages and types. Sue lives near the beach, just north of Brisbane, Queensland, with her granddaughter and a snarky cat, and still keeps in contact with RAF 514 Squadron.

Colorful smoke helps people on the ground follow the Roulettes' exciting movements in the sky.

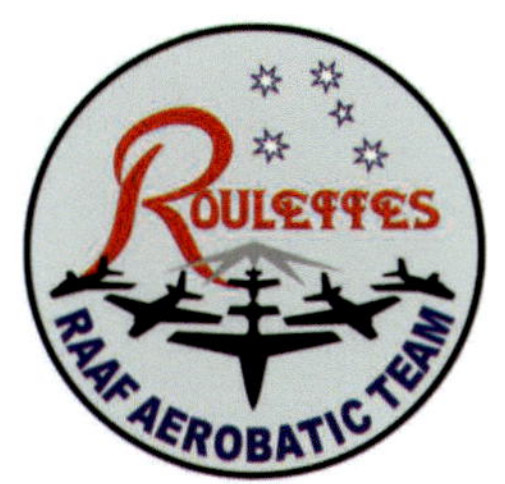


## CONTENTS



## WING TIPS

**The Roulettes' red, white, and blue colors reflect the pride and spirit of the Royal Australian Air Force (RAAF).** ↗

# Reaching for the Sky

A rumbling buzz in the distance gets closer and closer. It becomes a loud roar. It is the signal to look up. Six sleek scarlet shapes scream across the sky. Huge plumes of smoke trail behind them. The Roulettes have arrived at another event. Their real title is the Royal Australian Air Force Aerobatic Team.

Since their formation in 1970, the RAAF elite precision flying team has traveled back and forth across Australia, thrilling crowds everywhere. Their displays are a highlight of every event. Their skills show what the Australian Defence

Force Academy, the Air Force, and the Central Flying School (CFS) can offer young people.

The flying skills and moves of these highly trained jet pilots have become regular thrills at airshows, regional fairs, and other events. Loop-the-loops, barrel rolls, flips, corkscrews, and rollbacks are all part of their close formation routines. Their stunts show the skilled training each pilot brings to the squad.

The pilots are like pop stars. Fans line up for autographs, photos, caps, posters, and other items. Hundreds of kids walk away, imaginations fired up. They dream of the day when they might also achieve the heights of flying like a Roulette.

## PILATUS PC-21

The current aircraft of the Roulettes is said to be the most advanced pilot training jet in the world. The planes have air-conditioning to keep the pilot cool. The cockpit is pressurized. There is an anti-G system and on-board oxygen. The PC-21 gives trainee pilots the skills and knowledge to fly even more advanced aircraft, such as the F-35A Joint Strike Fighter. The PC-21 can maintain constant low-level speeds of more than 320 knots (368 miles/593 kilometers) per hour. Its top speed is 375 knots (432 miles/695 km) per hour.

**Pilatus PC-21** ↘

Smoke trails help people on the ground see the air displays.

A Gloster Meteor aircraft

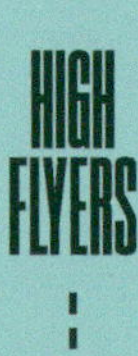

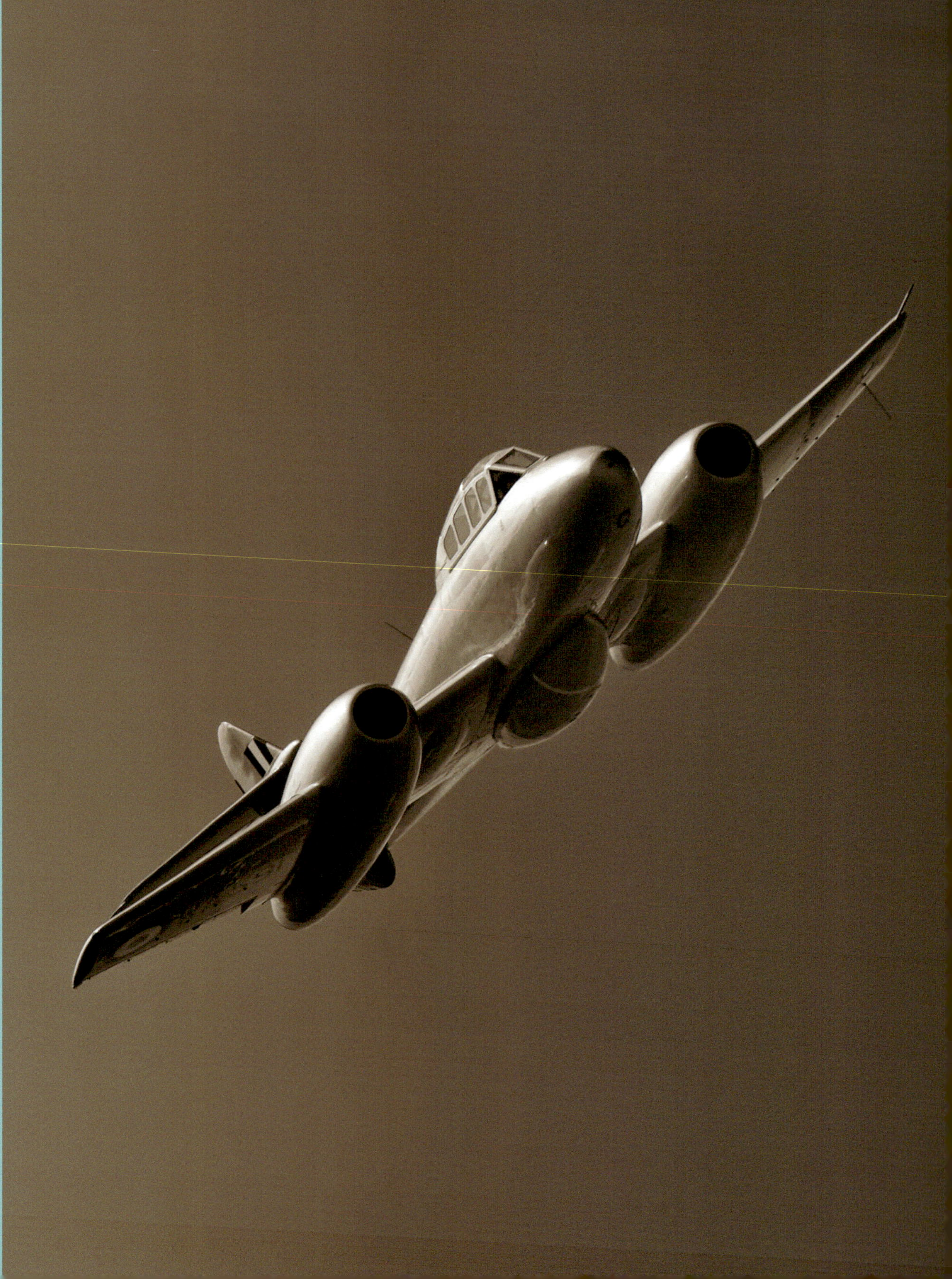

HIGH FLYERS

HIGH FLYERS

# The Flying Start

The history of Royal Australian Air Force air display teams goes back to 1956. The Meteorites, named for their Gloster Meteor F.8 craft, flew in a display at their base's Air Force Week in Williamtown, New South Wales. Their three planes were part of the No. 78 (Fighter) Wing. After 23 displays, the team was broken up.

The Central Flying School (CFS) at RAAF Base Point Cook was first set up in 1913 in Sale, Victoria. It created a team known as the Red Sales. This unit operated from 1962 to 1964. It flew five CAC CA-27 Mk.31 Sabres seconded from the No. 76

Squadron. A tragic crash killed four pilots and two passengers on a routine training. It abruptly brought this team to an end.

The CFS quickly regrouped. Wing Commander Herb Plenty formed a new team called the Telstars. He led this team himself. The team flew De Havilland Vampires. It performed its first display in February 1963. Air Commodore Brian Eaton was Plenty's successor. He guided the RAAF to replace the Vampires with the Italian-built Aermacchi MB-326 (also called Macchi). These planes could be built under license in Australia for less money. The Telstars flew their first Macchi display in February 1968. By April, the team was disbanded due to the RAAF cutbacks on display flying.

In 1970, the RAAF marked its 50th birthday. As part of this celebration, it created a new display team called the Roulettes. The name came from a figure performed in the air. The team has been permanent since then.

At first, the Roulettes were equipped with the Macchis used by the previous unit. Throughout the 1970s and 1980s, the squad switched between teams of four, then five, then up to seven and back down to five. Eventually, it was flying just two planes. These changes were the result of cost-cutting and issues developing with the fleet, mainly metal fatigue in the aircraft.

By the late 1980s, the Swiss-built Pilatus P-9 jets had started to arrive. In 1989, the Roulettes switched over completely to the seven-aircraft squad they have today.

The P-9 jets were replaced in 2019 by Pilatus PC-21 planes. They were painted in the team's striking red, white, and blue, with the letter "R" on each tail. In 2018,

## RED ONES GO FASTER

The early Roulette aircraft were red and white with the emblems of the RAAF and the Australian flag. The style had an old-fashioned feel, rather like World War II aircraft, except for the special "R" on the tail fin. In 2018, the PC-21s were given a complete makeover with modern styling. The new design kept some of the former look but added the Southern Cross stars. The different shades of red and blue, and the striking blue triangles that suggest the speed of the craft, took the look to a whole new level.

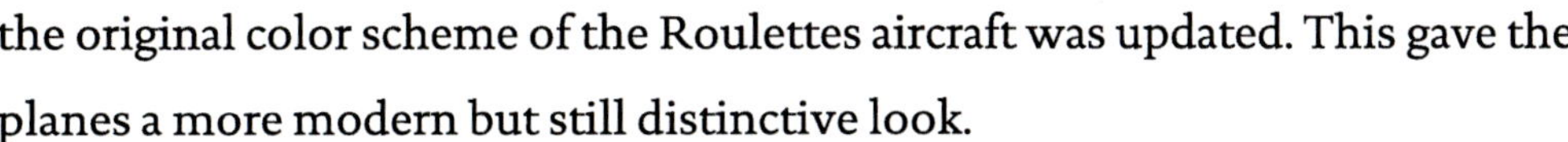

the original color scheme of the Roulettes aircraft was updated. This gave the planes a more modern but still distinctive look.

The Roulettes team is organized into "seasons" which run for six months. Most members fly three seasons before moving on again to other duties. The team has six members. Roulette One to Roulette Six are pilots. Roulette Seven handles non-flying duties. These include ferrying the spare plane to events. Roulette Seven does the talking at events and public relations. They organize appearances and other tasks. In their first season with the team, pilots fly as numbers two, three, or four. More experienced team pilots fly as numbers five and six, with the team leader taking the number one.

All pilots are trained flight instructors at the CFS. They have also served in other areas. They have all shown the superior skills and qualities necessary for this elite squad. The CFS senior instructors, along with the CFS commanding officer and the current Roulettes leader, will select individuals and invite them to try out for a place on the team. Being accepted into the Roulettes is a highly regarded achievement.

Joanne "Jo" Mein

## GIRL AIR POWER

In 1999, Flight Lieutenant Joanne "Jo" Mein entered the "her-story" books when she became the first female Roulette. She took up the number 3 (later number 6) position on the team. She wasn't just the first female in the squad's 29-year history. Mein was also the first woman on any military precision flying team. Fast forward to 2024 and Roulette Three. Flight Lieutenant Brodie Sweeney joined the Air Force in 2006. Sweeney has served in many operations in the Middle East and in humanitarian missions.

HIGH FLYERS

# Come Fly with Us

"And for all the boys and girls in the audience today, maybe one day you, too, could be a Roulette. Many of the Roulettes will tell you that they first made joining the team their goal when they were kids like you, watching one of our displays."

At any given event, Roulette Seven, as commentator, will make such a remark to the many youngsters in the crowd. After all, this is the primary purpose in maintaining the elite air display team. The RAAF is showing to possible recruits the opportunities the Defence Force, and especially the Australian Air Force, can provide.

Most of the Roulettes, past and present, will share that their fascination with flying goes right back to childhood. Former Roulettes leader, Squadron Leader Paul Henry (Roulette One, 2015) explained it was growing up in Traralgon, rural Victoria, that he first dreamed of flying. The local airfield was close. As young as five or six, he went with a friend to help wash helicopters and light planes. He would tell his parents how "awesome" a job being a pilot would be. He set his goals. He studied hard in school. He worked at McDonald's during high school to pay for flying lessons and got his pilot license—even before he got his driver's license!

Rather than studying at the Australian Defence Force Academy, Henry opted for a direct entry into the RAAF. After passing through flying school, he flew in various roles for more than a decade. Henry ended up back in Sale as a flight instructor. After a time, he joined the Roulettes team for two years. A posting away meant a break from the group, but then he was back. He was given the Roulette One leadership position. In his words, he was "not having as much fun as probably those guys are on the wing there, but it's certainly very rewarding."

Flight Lieutenant Aimee Heal (Roulette Seven, 2021) began her flight path at school when her father took her for a helicopter ride. She was hooked. She began taking lessons at the local aero club, gaining her student pilot license.

After completing a degree at the Defence Force Academy, Heal took on flying training. After graduating, she was posted to Townsville, Queensland.

As a newly qualified pilot, all her training, both practical and theoretical, was soon put to the test. The RAAF King Air she was flying lost its left engine

## SMOKIN'!

The billowing plumes of smoke following the Roulette jets are a thrill for many spectators. Smoke trails go right back to the 1950s. They were originally used for sign writing. The Roulettes planes have a special tank in what is really the baggage space. Smoke oil is pumped to the plane's exhaust from the tank. Sometimes the smoke is colored. This makes the display even more exciting for the crowd. The smoke also provides more safety in the performance. The pilots can more easily see each other in their formation.

completely. She stuck to the safety checklists and remained level-headed. It proved just how suited she was to her chosen path.

Heal said, "I definitely took away a lot from that experience." She remarked that the checklists are written for a reason. It doesn't matter how well a pilot knows them. When a pilot takes out the lists and goes through the action of reading them, it has a calming effect. This helps the pilot to get into a rhythm of how to deal with an emergency.

Heal had many deployments around the world, often managing the unwieldy Airbus A330 tanker with precision. Then, she was accepted into the Roulettes as their number seven non-flying member. She began her flight instructor training.

During shows, the planes sometimes fly super close—only 10 feet (3 meters) apart—in amazing tight formations.

HIGH FLYERS

# Straighten Up and Fly Fancy

After being selected for the Roulettes, pilots begin a three-month special training. The actual moves performed by the team are standard for any jet pilot. They differ from regular flying skills in two major ways. First is being able to do these moves with other planes, as a group. Second is doing the moves at a much lower altitude than usual.

A new Roulette starts with performing the simpler tricks of rolls and loops behind and to one side of another plane. This is called "flying in echelon." The Roulettes may also practice flying behind and below another plane—in "line astern." Then, they progress to the far more difficult exercises, such as ripple rolls, corkscrews, and rollbacks in "line abreast"—planes all in line with the leader. At last, they will work up to the full aircraft formations used in displays. Such exact moves require close focus.

Once these moves can be done perfectly, the next step is to reduce the altitude of the performance gradually. The new pilots practice this until the lowest safe level of 500 feet (150 m) is achieved.

Squadron Leader Mark Keritz (Roulette One, 2023) explained the preparation required for any event: "We have what's called a 'work-up' every six months." He went on to say that the team might have one or two members changing at any

## FUNCTION, NOT FASHION

The flying suits so familiar from Hollywood movies are daily wear for the Roulettes. For flying, the suit is khaki. Added is a G-suit, plus helmet with visor, oxygen mask, goggles, boots, foot straps, and earplugs. A G-suit is like an extra set of overalls, rather like waders. The G-suit has air bladders that plug into the plane. These fill with air and push against the legs and abdomen, while the pilot tenses their muscles against the suit. It prevents the blood pooling in the lower half of the body. Otherwise, it would push up into the upper body. The pilot would black out.

time. That could mean 30 to 50 work-ups to train people. It usually takes about six weeks, sometimes eight, to train people for a show.

Usually, this involves as many as 50 hours of flying time, to prepare for the average display of 10–15 minutes.

Many people might think of being a Roulette as a dangerous occupation. Actually, the tried and tested routines of any RAAF outfit mean the team has had a good safety record.

Of course, it has not been entirely without incident. But from 1970 to the present day, there have been only four accidents. Thankfully, only one was fatal.

Sadly, the first Roulettes accident was also the most tragic. On December 15, 1983, on a training exercise just outside Sale, two of the Macchi planes collided mid-air. Flight Lieutenant Steve Carter (Roulette Two) was killed instantly. Flight Lieutenant Graeme "Blue" Brooks (Roulette Three) fell from his plane as it fell to pieces and was able to parachute into a nearby swamp. He was air-lifted by helicopter to the district hospital. Unfortunately, while being treated, he suffered a cardiac arrest in hospital and died. It was a horrific moment for the team and for the families. There is now a monument to both these young pilots at the East Sale Air Force Base.

In 1988, another mid-air collision caused one pilot to eject, and the other to perform a gear-up landing. In 2005, a mid-air collision saw one pilot eject safely, and the other land his damaged aircraft. Most recently, in 2011, after an engine failure during training, one PC-21 crashed with the two pilots having safely ejected first.

The team practices many times a week to make sure their stunts stay safe and perfect. ↗

HIGH FLYERS

# Well Grounded

The Roulettes attend multiple events each year. It can be as many as 150 across Australia. Some are in friendly Southeast Asia countries. Some are major annual events like special services for Anzac Day and Australia Day. Others might be airshows or RAAF events. There are special celebrations in cities, for example, Riverfire in Brisbane, Queensland. Some, like the Australian Formula 1 Grand Prix, have displays over four days and attract worldwide attention. The preparation for a display means team meetings, planning, and creating schedules, alongside flying practice.

Because of the many events, it is sometimes easy to forget that the displays are not actually the pilots' main job.

Between training and attending events, the Roulettes and their aircraft are used in another role. Their main task is with the CFS. The team trains pilots to be flight instructors. Pilots already familiar with aircraft such as stealth fighters or heavy transport craft learn to fly the Pilatus PC-21s. A regular seven aircraft are reserved at any time for the Roulettes. There is also an entire fleet, 25 in total, based in Sale. They all have the same distinct red, white, and blue "uniform." For a pilot used to flying a Hercules transport, handling a PC-21 is like going from being a dump truck driver to a Formula 1 race car speedster. What a ride!

There are several methods of entry into the RAAF. Some will progress from Air Force cadets or the part-time Air Force Reserves. Others will make a choice after going to college. Still others will decide that they want better than their current job and look to a more rewarding opportunity. In general terms, an applicant must be an Australian citizen, at least 17 years old, who has completed at least junior high school. They should be fit and healthy. They need to pass all the medical and security checks.

An applicant might choose the direct entry officer-cadet route or apply to the Australian Defence Force Academy (ADFA) to study for a degree. They may already have a specialist degree, for example, medicine or dentistry, and apply for entry as an officer.

Watching the Roulettes fly inspires kids to learn more about planes, flying, and the Air Force.

Each Roulette pilot is a teacher who helps train new pilots for the Air Force.

## PAST TO PRESENT

In 2023, the Roulettes celebrated 50 years. Retired Air Vice-Marshal Frank Cox AO was a member of the first Roulettes team. He recalled "amazing teamwork, precision flying, and a great deal of discipline." He said he hoped the Roulettes would continue for another 50 years. He talked about the positive impact of displaying the skills of the members. The displays offer people an opportunity to see exactly what the Air Force can offer a person joining up. He finished by saying that is such a valuable way of promoting the RAAF to the public.

## The displays offer people an opportunity to see exactly what the Air Force can offer a person joining up.

Once accepted into the RAAF, new members choose the career path that best suits them. It could be a mechanic or a nurse. But for many, the sky is where they want to be. The RAAF has pilot programs at two bases. No. 2 Flying Training School is at RAAF Base Pearce, Western Australia. It is the primary pilot training school, flying the PC-21s. RAAF Base Williamtown, New South Wales, is Australia's prime fighter pilot training base. It is home to F-35A Joint Strike Fighter, Hawk 127, and PC-21 aircraft.

The next step for many trained pilots is becoming a pilot instructor. This is where the Central Flying School comes in. The CFS was founded in 1913 at Point Cook. As No. 1 Flying School, it moved across several locations before returning to the East Sale base. It has been the home of the Roulettes since the squad's beginning. The best of the best will advance their career at the CFS, with the most skilled being selected to join the Roulettes. Small wonder that the Roulettes are such a blazing spark to excite the next generation of RAAF members.

# INDEX